PaRables in action

Comet Campout

By Nancy I. Sanders and
Susan Titus Osborn

Illustrated by Julie Durrell

CPH
SAINT LOUIS

With love for my grandson Kolton. May you learn more about Jesus through reading this book. — S.T.O.

With love for Ben Shaner. May you continue to know Jesus more each day so that you'll "Be Prepared" to meet Him when He comes in all His glory. — N.I.S.

Parables in Action Series

Lost and Found
Hidden Treasure
Comet Campout
Moon Rocks and Dinosaur Bones

Text copyright © 1999 Nancy I. Sanders and Susan Titus Osborn
Illustrations copyright © 1999 Concordia Publishing House
3558 S. Jefferson Avenue, St. Louis, MO 63118-3968
Manufactured in the United States of America

1 2 3 4 5 6 7 8 9 10   08 07 06 05 04 03 02 01 00 99

Hi! My name is Suzie. My friends and I are going on a camp-out. We will hike in the hills. I'm waiting for my friends now.

Tonight a comet is going to race through the sky. I'm excited! I've never seen a comet before.

Here comes Mario and his dog Woof!

"Hi, Mario. It looks like you brought a big backpack today."

"I sure did, Suzie," Mario said. "I want to collect rocks on our hike. I need them for my collection."

Woof wagged his tail and barked. "WOOF!"

Just then Bubbles joined us. She had on a pink tutu. She looked like a ballerina. "You're wearing THAT on our campout?" I asked in surprise.

"Yes," Bubbles said. "I'm practicing for my next TV ad. I'm a ballerina."

Bubbles handed me her pink backpack. She twirled and did a pirouette.

Bubbles does ads on TV. She always practices for them.

"Here comes our teacher, Mr. Zinger," Mario said. "The only one missing now is The Spy."

Just then The Spy showed up.

"WOW!" I said. My mouth dropped open. The Spy carried the biggest backpack I'd ever seen! All sorts of junk poked out the top. It looked like he had EVERYTHING! Even a folding table.

"Larry, isn't that a bit much for a hike?" Mr. Zinger asked. Mr. Zinger always calls us by our real names.

The Spy shook his head. "Jickle, ee, ee," he said.

I knew what THAT meant. I'd been friends with The Spy a long time. "Jickle, ee, ee" was secret code for "Be prepared." The Spy talked in secret code. It looked like The Spy was pre-pared for ANYTHING.

"Let's go," Mario said. "I want to find some rocks."

We hiked through the park. We followed a trail up the hill behind the park.

Bubbles practiced three ballet leaps. R-I-I-P. Her pink tutu ripped on a bush.

"Oh, no!" she cried. "What will I do?"

We stopped.

The Spy took out his spy book and wrote notes. Then he reached in his backpack. He pulled out a needle and thread. He handed them to Bubbles.

"Jickle, ee, ee," he said.

"You're prepared, all right," Mr. Zinger said as Bubbles sewed the hole.

"Thanks," Bubbles said with a smile.